I Can Write

Written by Chemise Taylor

Copyright © 2020 by My Skills Books

Published by My Skills Books

All rights reserved. No part of this publication may be reproduced, distributed, or transmitted in any form or by any means, including photocopying, recording, or other electronic or mechanical methods, without the prior written permission of the publisher, except in the case of brief quotations embodied in critical reviews and certain other noncommercial uses permitted by copyright law.

First Printing, 2020.

ISBN: 978-1-951573-41-6

www.myskillsbooks.com

A

Pre-Writing Practice

Let's Write

Practice Makes Perfect

Apple   Ant   Alarm

a

Pre-Writing Practice

Let's Write

Practice Makes Perfect

at   and   as

B

Pre-Writing Practice

| | | | |)))))

Let's Write

BBBB

Practice Makes Perfect

Bread   Broom   Book

b

Pre-Writing Practice

| O | O | O | O | O | O

Let's Write

b b b

Practice Makes Perfect

be   bye   best

C

Pre-Writing Practice

Let's Write

Practice Makes Perfect

Carrot   Candy   Cloud

c

Pre-Writing Practice

⌒ c c c c c c c c

Let's Write

c c c c

Practice Makes Perfect

can   call   come

D

Pre-Writing Practice

|) |) |) |) |) |) |) |

Let's Write

D D D D

Practice Makes Perfect

Dream   Dress   Dog

d

Pre-Writing Practice

O | O | O | O | O | O | O | O |

Let's Write

d d d

Practice Makes Perfect

do   did   down

E

Pre-Writing Practice

Let's Write

Practice Makes Perfect

Earrings   Elephant   Egg

e

Pre-Writing Practice

Let's Write

Practice Makes Perfect

each   end   even

F

Pre-Writing Practice

Let's Write

Practice Makes Perfect

Feet   Fan   Fork

G

Pre-Writing Practice

Let's Write

G G G G

Practice Makes Perfect

Grapes   Glasses   Garage

g

Pre-Writing Practice

Let's Write

g g g g

Practice Makes Perfect

got   good   gone

H

Pre-Writing Practice

Let's Write

Practice Makes Perfect

Heart   Hat   Hand

h

Pre-Writing Practice

Let's Write

h h h

Practice Makes Perfect

here   have   how

I

Pre-Writing Practice

Let's Write

Practice Makes Perfect

Igloo   Ice   Island

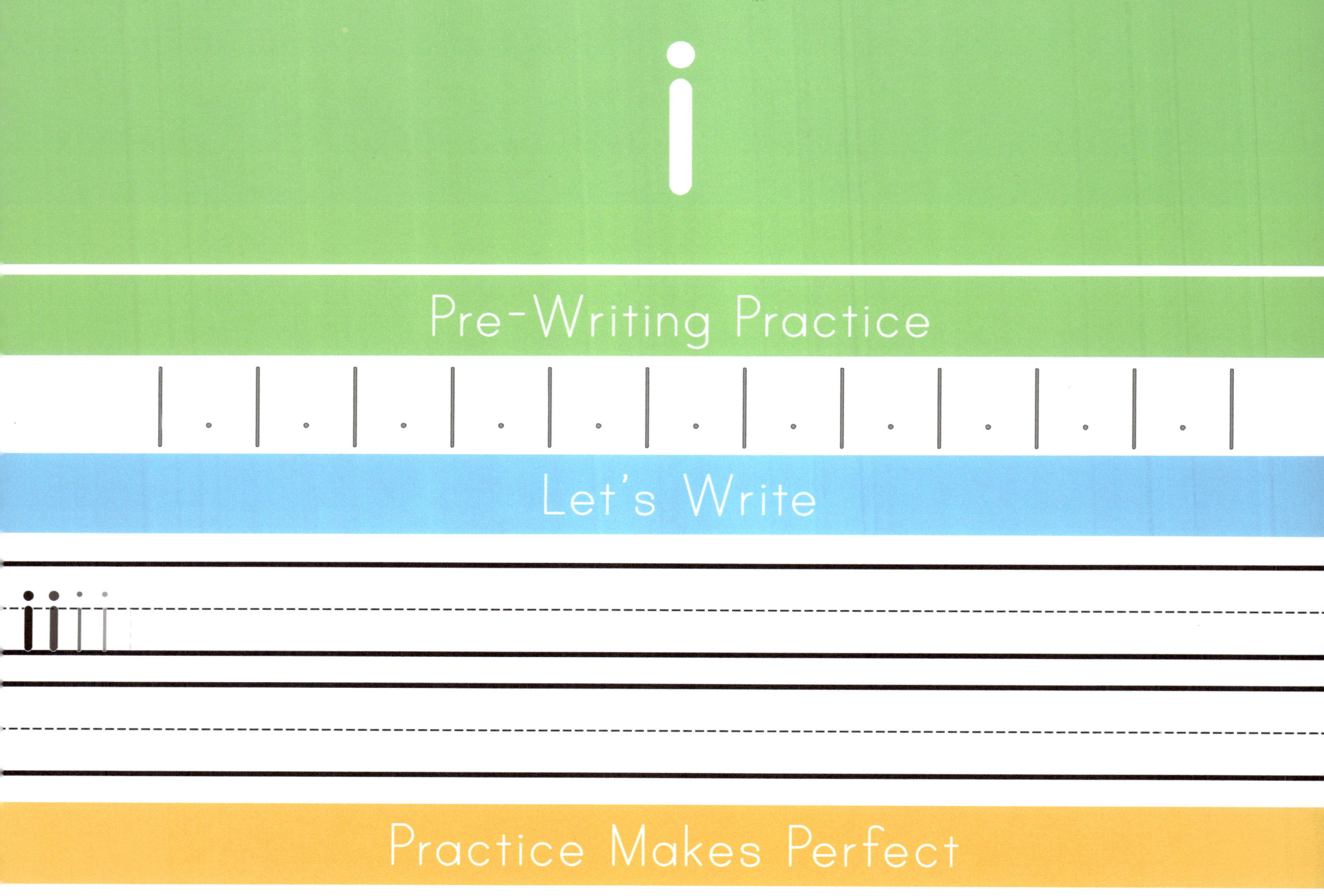

J

Pre-Writing Practice

Let's Write

J J J J

Practice Makes Perfect

Jet   June   Jar

K

Pre-Writing Practice

Let's Write

Practice Makes Perfect

Kite　　　Ketchup　　　Kangaroo

k

Pre-Writing Practice

Let's Write

k k k k

Practice Makes Perfect

keep know kind

M

Pre-Writing Practice

| | | | | | | \ \ \ \ \ / / / / /

Let's Write

M M M M

Practice Makes Perfect

Mouse   Milk   Money

m

Pre-Writing Practice

Let's Write

m m m

Practice Makes Perfect

meet   me   make

N

Pre-Writing Practice

Let's Write

Practice Makes Perfect

Necklace   Napkin   Notebook

n

Pre-Writing Practice

Let's Write

nnnn

Practice Makes Perfect

not   need   new

O

Pre-Writing Practice

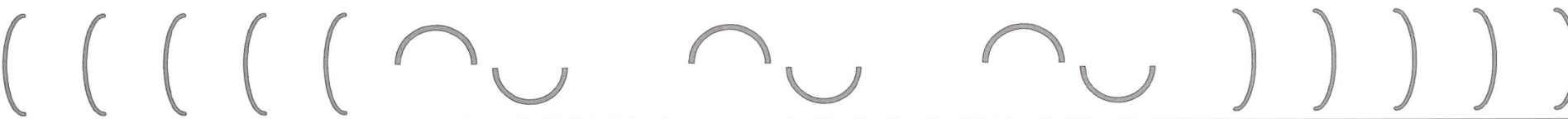

Let's Write

Practice Makes Perfect

Oven   Octopus   Orange

Pre-Writing Practice

○   ○   ○   ○   ○   ○

Let's Write

o o o o o

Practice Makes Perfect

f   ver   ld

P

Pre-Writing Practice

Let's Write

Practice Makes Perfect

Phone   Pencil   Piano

p

Pre-Writing Practice

Let's Write

Practice Makes Perfect

put   past   pull

Q

Pre-Writing Practice

Let's Write

Practice Makes Perfect

Quarter   Quilt   Queen

q

Pre-Writing Practice

Let's Write

Practice Makes Perfect

question　　　quiz　　　quiet

R

Pre-Writing Practice

Let's Write

Practice Makes Perfect

Rabbit   Remote   Roof

r

Pre-Writing Practice

Let's Write

rrrr

Practice Makes Perfect

red   right   rest

S

Pre-Writing Practice

Let's Write

S S S S

Practice Makes Perfect

Sun   Sandwich   Snake

S

Pre-Writing Practice

⌒ ⌒ ⌒ ⌒   \ \ \ \ \   ∪ ∪ ∪ ∪

Let's Write

SS S S

Practice Makes Perfect

so   sit   sad

T

Pre-Writing Practice

Let's Write

Practice Makes Perfect

Tent   Tiger   Table

U

Pre-Writing Practice

Let's Write

Practice Makes Perfect

Umbrella   Upstairs   Uniform

u

Pre-Writing Practice

Let's Write

Practice Makes Perfect

under up use

V

Pre-Writing Practice

\ \ \ \ \ \ \ \ / / / / / / / /

Let's Write

V V V V

Practice Makes Perfect

Vest　　　Violin　　　Vacuum

v

Pre-Writing Practice

\ \ \ \ \ \ \ \ / / / / / / /

Let's Write

v v v v v

Practice Makes Perfect

very   voice   vast

W

Pre-Writing Practice

\ \ \ \   / / /   \ \ \   / / /

Let's Write

W W W W

Practice Makes Perfect

Water   Watch   World

w

Pre-Writing Practice

\ \ \ \ / / / / \ \ \ \ / / /

Let's Write

w w w w w

Practice Makes Perfect

was   went   where

X

Pre-Writing Practice

\ \ \ \ \ \ \ / / / / \ \ \ \ \

Let's Write

X X X X

Practice Makes Perfect

X-ray   Xylophone   Box

X

Pre-Writing Practice

\ \ \ \ \ / / / / / \ \ \ \ \

Let's Write

xxxx

Practice Makes Perfect

ta x   fi x   mi x

Y

Pre-Writing Practice

Let's Write

Practice Makes Perfect

Yo-yo   Yogurt   Yarn

y

Pre-Writing Practice

\ \ \ \ \ / / / / / \ \ \ \ \

Let's Write

y y y y y

Practice Makes Perfect

yes   young   you

Z o

Pre-Writing Practice

- - - - - / / / / / - - - -

Let's Write

ZZZ

Practice Makes Perfect

Zero	Zoo	Zipper

z

Pre-Writing Practice

Let's Write

Practice Makes Perfect

zip   zoom   zone

Numbers

Let's Write

0 0 0 0

1 1 1 1

2 2 2 2

3 3 3 3

4 4 4 4

Numbers

Let's Write

5 5 5 5

6 6 6 6

7 7 7 7

8 8 8 8

9 9 9 9

www.ingramcontent.com/pod-product-compliance
Lightning Source LLC
Chambersburg PA
CBHW042111090526

44592CB00005B/86